The Power of Your
VISION

BECOME A VISIONARY AND
LIVE LIFE ON YOUR TERMS

The Power of Your VISION

BECOME A VISIONARY AND LIVE LIFE ON YOUR TERMS

JAKE WOODARD

ISBN 978-1975813215

Edited by Joy Dilworth
Author Photo: Steve Gallegos (www.steviegphoto.com)
Book Design by Joy Dilworth (www.joydilworth.com)

Printed and bound in the USA
First Printing October 2017

Published by CreateSpace.com

Visit the author's website at **www.jakewoodard.com** for more information about his mentoring services and speaking engagements.

Dedication

I'd like to dedicate this book to all those who have helped me along my journey. Words cannot describe how grateful I am. I would not be where I am today, if it wasn't for all of you.

Contents

Introduction

I want to start out by thanking you for reading this book with the desire to better the quality of your life. Most people will never take the time out of their "busy" lives to read a book that could potentially open their eyes to a new world and change their lives forever. Busyness rarely takes care of business. When you begin to seek answers you will find them, so my advice to you is to always be curious and continue to self-educate.

Do you feel like you have a lack of direction and purpose? Do you struggle with a lack of confidence and self-doubt? I can tell you that you are not alone and that many other people suffer from this, as well. Lack of direction and self-doubt cause many people to feel "stuck" in their lives. They want to live a better life, but they aren't sure how to create the vehicle that is going to get them there. Instead of looking for answers to this dilemma, they settle for an average and mediocre lifestyle. If you picked up this type of book, then I'm going to guess that this uninspiring lifestyle is not what you want and you are looking for more.

What is holding you back in your life? People are often held back by holding onto things that no longer serve them. This can be a job, a relationship, unhealthy eating, limiting beliefs, etc. One of the biggest things that people hold onto are toxic thoughts, which lead to unhappiness and stress, and stress is arguably the number one killer in our society. You cannot control what happens in your life. You can only control how you respond to that situation or event. The way you think about things is what becomes your physical reality, so how you choose to look at things also determines your level of success. Let me give you an example. If your goal is to lose one hundred pounds and you look at it just as that, then losing that one hundred pounds will probably seem like an impossible task to achieve. What if you were to look at it as losing ten pounds, ten times? That seems a little more realistic, right? This micro versus macro approach works the same way with your life goals and vision. If you say you want to become a millionaire and haven't even read a book on business or personal development, then that goal will also likely seem impossible. Before you invest into anything else, such as building a business or getting into a relationship, it's important to learn to invest in yourself first.

Everyone at some point in their life endures pain. How you use that pain will largely effect your level of success. You can either leverage that pain to push you to greatness, or you can become a victim of your own life. In the words of the great Tony Robbins, "Life happens for you, not to you." Don't become a victim of your own life. The people who create the most and have the biggest impact on our world are often those that experience the most struggles throughout life. Instead of conceding to a place of comfort, they use their pain to push them to new levels of achievement. What pain or suffering are you still holding onto that you could potentially turn into greatness?

I believe everyone has greatness within them and is capable of achieving anything they set their mind to. As soon as you become aligned with your purpose and your vision, you can begin to take action and set out to fulfill your life's work. Challenges that you used to face will seem like they don't exist anymore, or they will no longer be a struggle for you. It is so easy to get caught up in the "rat race" of life and to stay where it is comfortable. However, you will greatly limit your growth if you never push yourself out of your comfort zone. Without resistance, there is no growth. Think about how a plant grows. It has to push through the earth's surface, and when it arises, it has to face all of the elements trying to destroy it. This will also happen to you the more successful you become. When other people see you start to succeed in life, they will try to find flaws with what you are doing because your goals and dreams make them feel inferior inside. You are showing them what they gave up on in their life or never created for themselves.

Creating a compelling vision of your life—a vision so strong that when you hit adversity it will pull you through those hard times—is one key element to success that most choose to skip over. Becoming a visionary will allow you to begin to live life on your terms. I have spent thousands of hours studying successful people, reading personal development books, listening to audio recordings and attending seminars. Through overcoming my own challenges and adversities, I have learned how to embrace my discomfort and learned many helpful tools and strategies along the way. I want to share with you all that I have learned throughout my journey. *The Power of Your Vision* was written to help you create your vision, discover your life's purpose, unlock your full potential, breakthrough emotional barriers and build amazing relationships. My goal with writing this book is to show you that you too have gifts you can share with the world. Your gifts are already within you. They're just waiting for you to uncover them. So get ready, because we are about to embark on a beautiful journey of growth and achievement. After all, the entire world is waiting for you.

Chapter I

Our Journey Together

"You begin to fly when you let go of self-limiting beliefs and allow your mind and aspirations to arise to greater heights."

-BRIAN TRACY

Allow me to share with you a story about a boy named Jake Woodard. I grew up in a small country town, with a population of about five thousand people. I spent most of my childhood doing things that a typical boy shouldn't be doing. Lets just say I was a very destructive little boy. For some reason, I really enjoyed breaking things. I often heard the words, "Jacob! I can't believe you just did that!" from my mother. Lack of proper nutrition and discipline caused me to struggle with my weight as a kid, and I had serious issues with focusing because of an overabundance of energy. This lack of focus made me unable to channel my energy into doing anything productive.

When I was thirteen years old, I witnessed my

older sister stick a needle into her arm and instantly become addicted to the drug known as heroin. I was so confused and angry all in the same sense. I didn't know much about the drug, but I knew that it was highly addictive and it wasn't good. I had no way of knowing the amount of pain and suffering that I would endure over the next few years of my life. Have you ever been so overwhelmed by pain and anger that you just didn't know what to do, or experienced that clenching feeling in your throat because you are engulfed by that anger? That is the feeling I felt every single day for five years straight. I spent a long time in a dark place consumed by very negative thoughts. I had one of two choices to make. I could either play the victim role and hope that people felt bad for me, or I could start to make changes in my own life to begin to repair the damage. It was when I realized that no one really cares about your life, as much as you care about your life, that I started to take action. At that time, I had no idea how I was going to achieve greatness. I just knew that no matter what I was going to make this world a better place before I left it.

Within five years, I managed to get my health and fitness in check and lost over seventy pounds of fat and gained thirty pounds of muscle. I started reading books voraciously, developed an insatiable hunger for knowledge and new ways to help people. Through these incremental developments and getting my mind and body right, I discovered that I wanted to help people on a much deeper level. I knew I was willing to take their hand and guide them through depths of hell—down to the level where they are afraid to go alone—to show them the light. I share my story with you to show you what's possible, and that you too can turn your suffering or pain into an advantage. We all go through things in life, it's how you use those experiences that will determine the impact you will have.

Now that I have shared a piece of my life and become vulnerable with you, we are like family. It's in the moment that you are willing to open up that you will begin to receive blessings into your life. Allow yourself to become vulnerable and feel your emotions because vulnerability is power.

REMOVING LIMITING BELIEFS

When it comes to limiting beliefs, I know a thing or two about them because I too was consumed by them for a long period of my life. Over time, I've developed some strategies on how to remove them that I'm going to share with you. Before you can ever achieve any level of success or greatness, you are going to need to remove any limiting beliefs or self-doubt that you may have. Most people try to go out into the world and achieve success without first healing their own inner demons. If you haven't dealt with this issue first, it can make the process of achieving success very difficult, especially when you face adversity. Which if you haven't already faced some level of adversity in your life, you will at some point.

Our beliefs are mental notions and assumptions that we have about the world around us. They are psychological and emotional, and most of the time completely irrational—even though we look at them as being the absolute truth. What are your beliefs, and how are they shaping your life? So, now what is a limiting belief? A limiting belief is a negative thought that you have about yourself. This thought is again something that you believe to be the absolute truth.

Here are some examples of limiting beliefs:

- "I'm not good enough."

- "I don't deserve a better life."

- "What if I fail?"

- "What if other people don't accept me?"

- "I'm not smart enough."

The more energy you choose to give to these beliefs, the more they will continue to grow. Picture them having a snowball effect in your mind. The more energy that snowball receives, the bigger and stronger it becomes. When you are focusing on how bad you are at something or not believing in yourself, you will keep attracting exactly that. You want to allow your mind to focus on the beautiful things in life, not the bad. The only limitations that you have are those which you choose to acknowledge. Once you identify yourself in a particular way, that is who you are accepting you are and cannot change. For that reason, it's very important to be careful of the labels you place on yourself. For example, if you are struggling with losing weight, you cannot label yourself as a fat person. If you are broke, you cannot label yourself as being a broke person. If you are depressed, you cannot identify with depression. You have to see yourself better than you are in order to get where you want to be. Your mind has amazing abilities to create whatever you desire.

It is what you choose to focus on that becomes your reality. Let me give you an example of the power of focus. If you had a piece of paper and in the center of it was a black dot, what would you focus on? Most likely, it would be the black dot. It's small, but your eyes immediately go right to that dot. In life, that black dot is the negative; and all too often, it is easier for us to choose to focus on the negative and miss all of the positive things that we have. The reason why a laser can cut through a diamond and the flashlight on your phone cannot is because of the amount of focus that the laser has in one specific area. When you focus on how bad you are at something or why you can't do something, that gives power to that thought. Your focus should be on becoming self-aware and beginning to address those internal struggles that you are up against. When you become self-aware of the things you are saying to yourself, you will be able to start to eliminate anything that no longer serves you. Once you address a limiting belief, you can begin to replace it with a new empowering belief. This is done through, what is known as, neural reconditioning. You have to retrain your mind to think and believe positive thoughts. When a certain level of confidence is achieved and you've built internal strength, you will know that you'll become successful in whatever you decide to do. If you choose to ignore your weaknesses, they will show up at what seems like the worst possible moment and push you further down. These weaknesses pile up like trash in your mind and become toxic waste. It's important that you take the trash out and don't allow it to accumulate. You have to turn your weaknesses into strengths so that you aren't controlled by them.

What barriers have you created in your own life that won't allow you to move forward? Try to picture a mental roadblock that is stopping you from getting to where you want to be. Any roadblock or barrier, such as this, is not serving you and must be put under a spotlight. If you've only known a certain way of doing something your entire life, then it's often difficult to see things from a new perspective. This thought pattern is ingrained into your mind, and it will stay that way unless you learn how to break that pattern and replace it. In order to do that, you must be willing to receive new information. A lot of people have too much of their own information to receive anyone else's. When you are willing to stop being resistant, you will be able to receive other information that will help you. There is an African proverb that states, "A wise man never knows all. Only fools know everything." The goal is to change the way that you view the world around you. This all begins with changing the world within you because you can change your external environment but that won't do much good if you don't change your internal environment first. Everyone starts out with some level of doubt, but those that are most successful choose to address that doubt and turn their fears into energy.

Many of our limiting beliefs were formed in our childhood, due to the experiences that we had and our interactions with those around us. For example, think about how many times you were told, "No." as a child. By the time you are seventeen years old, you have likely heard the words, "No, you can't." an average of 150,000 times. You've also probably heard, "Yes, you can." on average about 5,000 times. That is a staggering thirty-to-one ratio! Imagine how powerful a belief that creates in your mind of telling yourself, "No." It's no wonder why so many people struggle with having self-confidence. Hearing, "No." that many times as a child creates a pattern in your mind of saying, "No." to yourself. You have to break that pattern and start saying, "Yes!" to yourself.

When you say it over and over again, it will become a habit. Repeating something daily is what makes a habit stick. We will talk more in Chapter 4 about how to develop habits that last.

If you were to build a car that was fueled on limiting beliefs, how long do you think that car would drive until it ran out of fuel? The car would be saying, "I can't do this. I'm not good enough." and "I will fail." Let's just say that you would be walking very soon. My question for you is this. Since you probably wouldn't build a car that is fueled by limiting beliefs, why do you keep fueling your mind with them? Your mind is the most powerful asset you have and can create whatever you desire in life, but it can only do so if you believe it's able to.

The fear of failure is one of the biggest limiting beliefs that holds people back. People are so afraid to fail at something, and it took me a long time to understand why because failure is arguably the best learning tool. When you fail at something, you only truly fail if you don't learn from your mistakes. What people struggle with is continuing to fail at the same thing over and over again throughout their entire life because they haven't learned anything from the previous failures. This is why you see people go from one relationship to the next with the same reoccurring issues. They will also gain and lose that same twenty pounds of weight over and over again. If you stubbed your toe on a chair so badly that it bled, would you go back to the same chair the next day and do it again? I'm guessing your answer would be, "No." because you learned the day before that if you do that again you will experience pain. The key is to stop stubbing your toe on the same chair in your life. When we associate pain with things that no longer serve us in our lives, we can begin to shift our perspective of the world around us. It's a matter of learning to step over or around the things that cause us pain. Humans assess situations one of two ways. They ask, "Will this bring me pain or pleasure?" By associating pain with the things that are blocking us from moving forward, we will no longer continue to keep doing the same undiscerning actions. What you want to do is to associate pleasure with things that are beneficial to you.

The conversations that you are having with yourself matter. There is always a conversation going on within your head. Those thoughts are indirect correlation with how you feel about your life. If a majority of those thoughts are negative or self-limiting beliefs, how do you think that is affecting your level of success and happiness? Thinking is some of the hardest work people can to do. That is why most people choose not to do it. When you raise your level of consciousness and have better thoughts about yourself, you will start having breakthroughs in your life. Having a higher level of consciousness is becoming more aware of the thoughts you are having and the things happening around you. I want you to develop positive self-talk and to achieve massive levels of success in your life. I want you to win. My question for you is this. Do you want all of that for yourself?

YOUR ACTION STEPS FOR THIS CHAPTER:

There are a few different ways you can remove limiting beliefs. I'm going to share with you one way that I found to be very powerful. Understand that like anything else, this isn't going to be solved overnight and must be done consistently in order to be effective. Patience is a real key factor here. You must first become aware of the limiting beliefs that you are having.

Take out a pen and piece of paper, or use the lines below. Write down three limiting beliefs that you have about yourself. Take some time, and really challenge yourself to think about this. When something shows up, write it down.

Identify three limiting beliefs that have been producing negative or unwanted consequences in your life.

1. _____
   _____

2. _____
   _____

3. _____
   _____

Now that you have identified your limiting beliefs, it's time to create your new empowering beliefs. Write down your old limiting belief, cross that out, and below it write your new empowering belief.

Example(s):

Limiting Belief: "I'm not smart enough"

Empowering Belief: "I am confident in all that I do!"

1. _____
   _____

2. _____
   _____

3. _____
   _____

Chapter 2

Creating Your Vision

"If you are working on something exciting that you really care about,
you don't have to be pushed. The vision pulls you."
-STEVE JOBS

If you are intending to build something amazing in your life, you must first envision it being built in your mind. Your mind must arrive at your destination before your life does. What thoughts do you often have that you want to manifest into your life? If you feel that you struggle with lack of direction or purpose, then I can totally relate. For a majority of my life I had no vision. I had big dreams and goals, but I could never visualize myself actually achieving any of them. It was when I learned about the idea of creating a vision that things became more clear and ideas started to flow freely.

There is something known as the *Law of Attraction*. The reason why it's called a law is because it is just that. Summed up simply, what you put out to the universe is exactly what you will receive back. This can work both for the good and the bad in life. It will have a "boomerang effect." Picture yourself throwing a boomerang and it coming back to you. It works the same way with your thoughts and what you attract into your life. This is not an instant return, and no one knows exactly when what you attract will come back to you. It could be instant, days, weeks, or even years before it does. If you are constantly putting out negative thoughts and vibrations, then you will receive negativity into your life. If you put out positive thoughts and vibrations, you will receive positivity. If you want to attract love into your life, then you must first be willing to give love. If you want to attract more money, then you must be willing to give away money with positive feelings attached to it. Basically, put a mirror up to your face and really study what you are putting out to the world.

I know to some people that might seem kind of out there, and that's exactly what I thought when I first heard of this concept. I can tell you from my own experiences that this is very real. Everyone believes in the *Law of Gravity*, that states what goes up must come down. If you decide to test out this law by jumping off of a building (which I don't suggest you doing), you will feel real pain. Why then is it so difficult to believe in the Law of Attraction? If you are interested, there is a great book called *The Secret* by Rhonda Byrne that explains this in more depth. Reading this book will help you to understand why you should change your negative thoughts to positive thoughts. By switching your thoughts from negative to positive and becoming conscious about what thoughts you are having, you can begin to control your thoughts. You first must become aware of the thoughts you are consistently having.

Take a look around you right now. You have created everything in your life based on your thoughts. Thoughts can bring you immense happiness, or they can bring you insufferable amounts of pain and anger. The thoughts that bring you happiness are the ones you want to begin to create more of. Figure out why something made you happy in the first place, then just rinse and repeat. It is possible to become happy most of the time, regardless of what you have been conditioned to believe. On average, we have around 60,000 thoughts a day, and these thoughts create your world. If a majority of those thoughts are negative, how do you think it will impact the quality of your life?

VISUALIZE YOUR GREATNESS

Plenty of stories throughout history tell of how positive thinking alone took people out of a bad place or brought them to new levels of achievement. Some tell of people having been on their death beds and just by thinking positive thoughts over and over again they managed to overcome a fatal ailment. There are also a number of stories of well-known individuals, all of which are the best or greatest in their respective fields, that envisioned their success and greatness before it actually became real.

Here are some examples of such individuals:

- **Muhammad Ali**, who some would say is the greatest boxer to ever live, visualized himself becoming the world's greatest boxer long before he was ever at that level. "I am the greatest," he would say.

- **Tiger Woods**, one of the best golfers to ever live, has used visualization ever since he was a little boy by visualizing exactly where he wants the golf ball to go.

- **Arnold Schwarzenegger**, one of the best bodybuilders to ever live, four-time Mr. Olympia, and five-time Mr. Universe, has not only used visualization for athletic success but also credits it for his success as a movie star. He has said, "When I was very young I visualized myself being and having what it was I wanted. Mentally, I never had any doubts about it."

- Billionaire **Oprah Winfrey**, who is known internationally for her talk show, television network and publishing empire, has mastered the art of envisioning her success. She said it best: "Create the highest, grandest vision possible for your life because you become what you believe."

- A few other successful people that have used visualization to bring their dream to life are **Micheal Jordan**, one of the best basketball players to ever life; **Mark Zuckerberg**, the co-founder of Facebook; and **Sara Blakely**, who is an American billionaire businesswoman and founder of Spanx.

Have you noticed a common thread here? When you see the historical amount of impact that visualization really has on people that have done incredible things, it's easier to believe. Now I know that some people may be reading this and saying, "Yeah, that's just luck or coincidence." Me personally, I stopped believing in luck and coincidence after I started studying these universal laws and things started happening in my own life. Learning about all of these people that were able to see success before it was real has been very empowering and reaffirming to me.

Understand that creating your vision and becoming clear on what you want to achieve is one of the most foundational components of becoming successful. It takes, effort, consistency and patience, but once you become clear you can bring it into reality. Look at your vision like a GPS, and I'm sure at some point in your life you have used a GPS to get to your destination. If you haven't, you have probably used a map. These tools exist to guide you to where you want to go. Your vision is going to be the tool that is your life's roadmap. Make sure you pay close attention to this map.

If you are desiring to quit smoking cigarettes, start a business, lose weight, make more money, or find your dream partner, you must first be able to see it as if it was already real! You can't hit a target you can't see. Think about this. If you were given a bow and arrow to hit a target and put up against one of the top archers in the world, who would hit the target more times? Most likely the top archer, right? What if that same archer were now blindfolded? Your odds of hitting the target are now much better than theirs because you have vision! People that don't have a vision won't have anything strong enough to help motivate them when they face adversity. This vision that you have created, will help pull you through when you hit that wall. Many people struggle to create a vision or just skip this part of the process. I know creating a vision for me was a real struggle because I love opportunity and always wanted everything all at once. You may struggle with this symptom, as well, but I advise you to not skip this step! Take however long you need to get crystal clear on what you want in life. Once you figure out a good idea of what you want, then begin taking action.

Create what is called a vision board where you cut out pictures of everything you want in your life. It could be things like a nice house, philanthropy work, being on the cover of a magazine or a nice car. Whatever you desire, put it on this board and look at it daily. When you look at the pictures, it's important to feel as if it's already real. Remember, this is your dream life, so design it however you want. If your dreams and aspirations don't scare you a little bit, dream bigger. Inevitably, you will have people laugh when you tell them about all of the things you want to accomplish. That's okay because they won't be laughing when you accomplish these things. They will come to you and ask how you were able to create all of that in your life.

One of my mentors, Rod Khleif, uses the practice of creating vision boards for things he has wanted in his life; and I have been fortunate enough for him to share them with me. He has managed to achieve about 90 percent of the things on his boards, and these weren't little things either (an eight million dollar mansion on the ocean, a Lamborghini, a non-profit organization for children and a beautiful, loving wife)! All things he was able to create because he visualized them into his life!

There is a part of your brain known as the Reticular Activating System (RAS). This is your brain's attention center. Have you ever wondered why, when you wanted a specific car, you started seeing that exact car everywhere? That car was always really there, but you just started noticing it more because your RAS was seeking it out. When we start seeking something, our minds have an innate ability to find what we are looking for. You just have to be conscious enough to know when it shows up. There is so much power in the saying, "Seeing is believing." If I had not physically seen Rod's vision boards, I would have been very skeptical. Just as you may be, as you're reading this. You should know that along with being able to see your vision, you must also feel as if your vision is already real in order for it to take shape.

Another form of visualization is goal setting. Writing your goals down with pen and paper can help you bring those goals into fruition. The act of writing down a goal anchors that thought to your subconscious mind. I recommend that you plan out your goals by writing them down weekly and reviewing them daily. You should be very specific with the details of these goals and the date you want to achieve them by. Then run your fingers over those goals, and say them out loud as you do this. These techniques will only work if you take action and start now. Once you start visualizing what you want your life to be like and believing it, doors will start opening up for you.

YOUR ACTION STEPS FOR THIS CHAPTER:

There are three questions that I want you to answer in order to help you create a vision. Write your answers below or on a separate sheet of paper, and share them with someone that will keep you accountable!

1. What do you believe that you could become the best in the world at?

   _____

   _____

2. What consumes most of your thoughts to the point you cannot stop talking about it?

   _____

   _____

3. What makes your heart sing?

   _____

   _____

Chapter 3

Overcoming Fear

What pops into your mind when you hear the word fear? Let's take a moment and get clear on what fear actually is. Fear, by definition, is "an unpleasant emotion caused by the thought that someone or something is dangerous and likely to cause pain or be a threat." Our two million-year-old brain was developed to protect us from saber-toothed tigers and to fight for our survival. You have to be able to distinguish the difference between a real danger and something your mind is creating based off of your current emotional state. In most cases, the fear you are "feeling" is made up. Remember, "feeling" is an emotional state, not your current reality.

The part of your brain, known as the amygdala,

is responsible for the "freeze, fight or flight" mechanism. Every time you get upset or have what is known as a "neural highjacking", the amygdala is at work. The chemical norepinephrine is released during these times of stress or danger, and it's designed by your body to protect you. This chemical mobilizes the brain and body into action, and this is the reason why most people who are constantly stressed are burned out! On average, it can take up to 24 hours time to recover from just one of these stressful situations. This is what is often referred to as someone "burning a candle at both ends." This ongoing stress will cause adrenal fatigue, due to the fact that you are constantly stimulating your adrenals for no rhyme or reason. What is the lesson here? Remain calm, and learn to use the rational part of your brain instead of the emotional part. It's been said that when your emotions are controlling your thinking, it's a 24:1 ratio. Emotion (24), rational thinking(1). That's a pretty dominant ratio, seeing as how you should always try to be a rational thinker! Irrational thinking is when you are being irate, meaning not logical or reasonable. One of the main reasons most people never become successful is because of their fear of failure. The fear of failing has killed many amazing dreams and visions because it caused the people with them to never take action. By simply taking action—even when it's small action—you begin to kill fear.

When you begin your journey of growth and achievement you will most likely have a bunch of "what ifs" pop into your mind. "What if I'm not good enough?" "What if I'm not smart enough?" "What if I get rejected?" "What if I fail?" Do any of these sound familiar? Are you the type of person that over analyzes every situation and ends up just not taking any action at all? This is what is known as "analysis paralysis." People who are too analytical miss opportunities because they actually paralyze their thought process. This is why it is important for you to focus in on what you really want to accomplish. Bring all of your focus to that area in order to be able to master it. Don't be a person who just dabbles with different things and never masters anything. Confucius once said, "He who chases two rabbits, catches none." When you haven't invested enough time into growing your mind, those thoughts will keep you in exactly the same spot your whole life.

Our society conditions us to be fearful and live with a scarcity mindset. This is why every time you turn on the news, radio or any other form of media, the majority of the content you see is negative. They are conditioning you to believe that the world we live in is a terrible place! When in reality, we are living in a time with more opportunity than ever before in history. It is important that you stand guard at the gate of your mind and don't allow negativity to penetrate it.

When a person has an underdeveloped mindset, they are very easily influenced. This is often why you see people change when they are around certain people. They do this because they're unsure of who they are and have no direction in their own life. They haven't taken the time to develop a vision that will guide them.

Being afraid to fail is a natural feeling, but you don't have to allow it to control your life. Look at it as just a seed being planted in your mind. The more you water that seed, the more it will grow. If you plant a "fear" seed in your mind and continue to water it with affirming negative thoughts, it will grow stronger and stronger. The point is, make sure you are only planting seeds in your mind that can grow positive thoughts. Don't feed into your fears, or else they will keep you held back. There is a well-known acronym for fear, **F.E.A.R.** or **False Events Appearing Real.** I choose, however, to see this acronym as meaning **Face Everything And Rise.** Ninety-nine percent of the fear that you have in your mind is that which you have created, and it can only be real if you believe it to be. It's said that the richest place in the world isn't China, nor Dubai; it's the graveyard. There lay dreams that were never brought to reality because fear killed those dreams. When you come to the end of your life, you don't want to have a long regretful list of things you should have achieved but didn't because you were too afraid to just take action.

TURN YOUR STRUGGLES INTO STRENGTH

Every successful person, at some point in their life, faces the fear of failure. Overcoming that fear, by taking massive amounts of action and "failing their way to success", is what enables these same people to achieve at such high levels. Thomas Edison's teachers told him he was "too stupid to learn anything". He then went on to invent the electric lightbulb. He was criticized for failing 10,000 times during his effort to make the lightbulb work. However, his response to those critics was, "I did not fail at lighting the lightbulb 10,000 times. I successfully learned what did not work 10,000 times." Then after the invention of the lightbulb, Edison went on to hold over 1,000 patents and also create some of the most world-changing devices.

It's been said that Colonel Harland David Sanders, best known as Colonel Sanders and the founder of KFC, was turned down over 1,009 times before his world famous fried chicken recipe was first accepted. On top of that, he also started his business at 65-years-old, an age when most people begin their retirement. What enabled him to keep going was that, with every failure, he kept on changing and refining his approach. He knew exactly what he wanted and just kept taking action. KFC is now one of the world's most recognizable franchises, with over 18,000 international locations.

Walt Disney, the founder of the Disney empire, was fired at the age of 22 from a newspaper company in Missouri for "not being creative enough." He was rejected over 300 times by bankers who thought his Mickey Mouse idea was absurd. The Walt Disney Company is now one of the largest media and entertain corporations in the world in terms of revenue.

Do you notice a common theme amongst these people who have achieved such massive amounts of success? They didn't give up after they failed at something the first time. They kept pushing until they broke through that barrier to success. Most people give up too soon, and it's usually just before they have that major breakthrough in their life. They don't make the effort to build up their resiliency muscles, and when they fail at something, they just give into that failure and go right back to where they are comfortable. This is why people stay stuck where they are in life and don't experience much growth.

Do you remember when you were a little kid and learned how to ride a bike? You most likely didn't just hop on and ride off without falling down multiple times first. When you started learning, you were probably wobbly; but when you fell down, you got back up because you were determined to learn how to ride that bike. The fear of failing doesn't naturally exist in a child's mind because they haven't been conditioned by society or their surroundings to be fearful yet. In your life now, you are probably a lot more cautious and afraid of failure because of years of negative conditioning. There is, however, a difference between just taking risks and allowing for calculated risk; and the more that you invest in yourself, the easier it will become to determine the level of risk factor to allow for each situation.

Another way you can deal with managing fear is by acknowledging it every time it shows up in your life. Picture yourself sitting in your house and fear opens up the door. Now you have one of two options to choose from; you can either run and hide from your fears, or you can stand up and embrace them. I want you to dance with your fear. I know, at first, this is going to be uncomfortable; but when you feel that fear overcome you, take a step forward. Put yourself into a continual state of action. The more you continue to take action and face your fear, the more those fears will begin to die away. If you just keep running from your fears, they will always continue to show up. Each time you step forward into fear, you are building up your resiliency muscles. In the same way that you train a muscle in the gym, the more resistance and pressure you put on it, the more that muscle will to grow. Strength is also developed through repetition, so the more you use your resiliency muscles the stronger they will grow. You want to always be growing your mind muscles and strengthening areas where you are mentally weak. Build a "six-pack" for your mind.

What is the purpose of dreaming of something, if you aren't going to make it come true? If it makes you feel good when you're thinking about it, why not bring it to life? I'm here to tell you that whatever you can dream, you can achieve. When you set your mind to something, no amount of fear will hold you back. You will do whatever it takes to break through that threshold to get there.

YOUR ACTION STEPS FOR THIS CHAPTER:

Take out a pen and paper, or use the lines below to write down every fear you have right now that you believe is holding you back in your life. Is it the fear of failure, the fear of money, the fear of rejection?

Once you have written all of them down, it's time to remove them by asking yourself new questions. Every time one of these fears show up, ask yourself one of these questions.

1. What is the worst that can happen?

   _____

   _____

2. What would this feel like, if I wasn't afraid?

   _____

   _____

3. How much is it costing me to not take action?

   _____

   _____

Chapter 4

Stay True to the Process

Habits are what you consistently do on a regular basis. In order to develop good habits, you must practice them often. There are two types of habits. Those that serve you, and those that don't. Some examples of positive habits are: reading inspirational books, going to the gym, connecting with like-minded people, and having positive self talk. Some examples of negative habits are: eating unhealthy foods in excess, complaining, avoiding your issues, and having negative self-talk.

I want you to take a moment and think about what habits you currently have. How are those habits affecting you? Over time, those habits become a part of who you are; and your life will be defined by these habits. Think of habits like a rocket-ship taking off from the Earth's surface. When it takes off, it has to use massive amounts of energy to get off the ground. However, when it gets into space, it can use its momentum to carry the rocket-ship huge distances.

Once you have repeated them enough times, these habits will be set on auto-pilot and become an unconscious act. There is a system in our brain, known as the psycho-cybernetic mechanism, which is the brain's "auto-pilot". This system is designed like a cruise control for your brain. Picture yourself on the highway, driving in your car. When you place your car on cruise control, you no longer need to think about the speed at which you're traveling. Your car is programmed to continue traveling at the same speed, until you switch it off. Think about all of your habits that are programmed into your mind, and that you do without even thinking about them. Every time you try to take on a new habit, your brain's psycho-cybernetic mechanism will try to switch back over to cruise control. This is due to your brain's programmed neural circuits, and is one of the main things that keep people stuck doing the same routines. In order to develop new habits, you must first consciously become aware of the habits you already have programmed within you. Once you have identified your current habits, you can begin to shift them to reprogram as new ones. If you begin to develop proper habits, the quality of your life will change within months.

I've read many different articles on how long it takes for a habit to stick and become a part of your life. Most people think it's 21 days, but it's actually quite a bit longer than that. How long then do you have to maintain discipline in order for your new behavior to become automatic or engrained? The point is to reach "automaticity", which on average takes 66 days to form a new habit.

When developing new habits, it's best to focus on them individually. No one really has the power to effectively develop more than one at a time. You want to build a few powerful habits, over the course of time. This will have a compounding effect.

THE POWER OF COMPOUNDING

If you were given the option of choosing between one million dollars now or a penny doubled everyday, for 30 days, what would you choose? Ninety-percent of people would most likely choose the million dollars now. Without the understanding of compounding, this is a common choice. If you chose the million dollars now option, you lost out on a little over four million dollars. Here's why. The simple act of doubling your previous days investment can radically reap huge rewards thanks to the power of compounding. A penny doubled everyday leads you to a sum of $5,368,709.12. I bet you're reconsidering taking the first option of a million dollars now, right?

What does this have to do with your habits? By making a small investments each day into your positive thought bank account, it will lead to great results over time. Doing small actions, daily and consistently, will eventually lead you to success. Just think about your positive actions being the penny doubled everyday for 30 days straight.

When I was struggling to lose weight, I kept focusing on how fat I was. I wasn't focused on taking small actions everyday to lose the weight. When I shifted my perspective and realized I could lose one to two pounds a week through proper nutrition and exercise, I started to see results over the course of just a few months. I couldn't believe that I was finally starting to become fit and love the way my body looked! I had to first develop a new habit of the way I thought about my body. Once I changed my thinking about my body, then I started to think differently about the foods I was consuming. I began to ask myself questions like, "Is this food clogging or cleansing me?" It's important to ask yourself better questions because that will help you to get better answers.

Once we start becoming conscious and aware of the things that are no longer serving us, we can start to change them slowly over time. The reason why you see a lot of people fall on their faces, when they try to change something, is because they try to do it all at once. They want what is known as "instant gratification". So many of us desire immediate results or the "quick fix". You see a lot of this, today, in the marketing world. "Come sign up for my program, and change your life in thirty days!" You also see a lot of get rich quick schemes. "Make a million dollars in 6 months, working from home!" These are just some examples of things you may have seen or something similar to them. The point is that marketers are preying on the masses to tempt them with the promise of instant gratification, when they know it's not really possible. They see an opportunity to make money off of a person in need and who is wanting to change their life. I, personally, don't agree with these tactics because it's false hope. We live in a clickable world today. You can go on the internet to click and buy just about anything you want, and you'll have it within a couple of days. Building your dream life is a lifelong process within itself. You must commit to the process and fall in love with that process. The strongest standing structures are the ones that are built with the best foundations underneath.

If you were going to build a house, you would first want to dig a hole deep into the earth and pour a solid concrete foundation. This would be done before you began framing the actual structure of the house. It wouldn't be advisable to just build a house on the Earth's surface because it would collapse without the proper support underneath it. Many people are building their lives like houses without a strong foundation underneath them. They just skipped the pouring of a concrete foundation and went right into the construction of the home. They were too impatient to build something substantial enough to hold up against strong winds or the constantly shifting earth. This is why they say, "Patience is a virtue."

When you observe your habits, look at them like building a strong foundation for your life. You want to develop habits that will serve you and will be able to guide you when things get hard on your journey.

When you are addicted to a feeling of instant gratification, it can be very difficult to break that habit.
This can show up in many different forms such as
drugs, sex, money, alcohol and food. These forms of
quick pleasure attach strongly to who you are and become a part of your everyday life. I will tell you that
instant gratification will never bring you long-term
fulfillment or happiness.

If you gave a person a bowl of ice cream and then
hooked them up to an FMRI (Functional Magnet-
ic Resonance Imaging) machine, which measures
brain activity by detecting changes in blood flow, you
would see a temporary increase in their level of happiness because of the release of dopamine and sero-
tonin into their blood stream. They are associating
pleasure with the sugar in the ice cream. Then after
10-15 minutes, their happiness levels go back down
to normal; and they feel exactly the same as they did
before the ice cream. Did that bowl of ice cream really bring that person happiness? No. It only brought
them a temporary feeling of fulfillment.

Are the habits you have in your current life bring-
ing you lasting fulfillment or happiness? Would you
say that most of them are just forms of instant gratification? It's easy for us to go after a quick fix or in-

stant shot of happiness, but it never last. The goal is to build habits that will bring you lasting happiness. When you are able to understand that a habit is a thought that has been ingrained into your mind by repetitive action, you can change them or develop new ones.

Think about when you got out of bed this morning. You probably didn't even think twice about putting your pants on or brushing your teeth before you left your house. You did those acts without even thinking about them. Those are what are known as unconscious acts, meaning that your mind does them automatically without having to think about it. Imagine how powerful it would be to have your mind automatically seek doing things everyday that improved your level of wealth, love, happiness or health? Put your mind on autopilot to become success conscious.

When you become obsessed with the process and are always seeking improvement in all areas of your life, you will continue to grow. The journey you are on is life-long, but that journey begins with a single step forward. Don't become so focused on getting a specific result because when you get there it might not be what you expected. Enjoy the process you have to go through in order to get results, and always have your next goal lined up.

YOUR ACTION STEPS FOR THIS CHAPTER:

Write down your answers below or on a separate sheet of paper.

1. Write down all of the habits you have that serve you.

_____

_____

_____

_____

_____

_____

2. Write down all of the habits you have that no longer serve you.

_____

_____

_____

_____

_____

_____

3. What are some new habits that you could develop to get you to your goals faster?

_____

_____

_____

_____

_____

_____

CHAPTER 5

Your Circle of Influence

"Surround yourself with the dreamers and the doers, the believers and the thinkers, but most of all, surround yourself with those who see the greatness within you, even when you don't see it yourself."

-EDMUND LEE

I am a strong believer in having great people within your circle of influence. The reason why its called a circle of influence is because you are "influenced" by the people you are surrounded by. Jim Rohn said it best: "You are the average of the five people you surround yourself with the most." When you are around someone, you are giving and receiving vibrational currencies. That's why, if you've ever been in a room and someone entered and they were in a really bad mood, you quickly noticed that person being upset. How many people in your life would you say are positive, and how many are negative? What type of people do you associate with? If you take a look at the people you are closest with, I bet you're within the same class of people as they are. If you're not, then it may be time to upgrade the level of people in your life.

A lot of people will choose to complain about their circumstances, but they don't want to do anything to change them. They can find a flaw in absolutely anything. I want you to become conscious about who you are associating yourself with. They are influencing you right now, whether it's for good or bad. Understand that when you complain to someone, 95 percent of the people don't care about your problems, and the other 5 percent are glad that they happened to you. Are you starting to understand the power of association, yet?

Here are some examples of the impact your circle of influence can have on you:

- If you associate with five smart people, you will become the sixth.

- If you associate with five morons, you will become the sixth.

- If you associate with five rich people, you will become the sixth.

- If you associate with five broke people, you will become the sixth.

When you're in a relationship with someone and your values aren't in alignment, there is a good chance that relationship will end up failing. If you're all about health and fitness, reading, networking and success, but your significant other wants to go out and get drunk all of the time, then you probably aren't aligned. It's important that you find someone you share similar values with. I see a lot of people struggle with what I refer to as "shiny rock syndrome." You see someone's physical image, and you become instantly attracted to them. If all that you share with someone is physical attraction, there's a good chance it won't last. You need to go below the surface level to build a real connection with them. Picture a person like they're an ocean. The ocean is up to seven miles deep in some areas, but the waves are only on the surface. It's important that you explore below those waves, before getting deeply involved with someone.

You can gauge a person by the size of a problem that gets them down. If a small problem arises, and they lose their mind; it gives you a good indication of how that person is going to respond to problems during the course of your relationship. Don't be naive enough to think that there won't be some problems to face as the relationship progresses. Even the strongest relationships have problems, but it's the way the partners choose to deal with those problems that make them successful. When you start to become more aligned with who you are and what your purpose in life is, you will attract better people into your life. The better that you become, the better those you will attract into your life will be.

Why do people choose to stay in toxic and unfulfilling relationships? Just staying with someone for comfort or out of the fear of them being with someone else is a selfish act towards both yourself and the other person. This also happens with friendships, business partners, and family members. There are about 7.5 billion people on this planet. If it doesn't workout with someone, there are plenty of other people out there you will align with. Don't allow someone to become comfortable with disrespecting you. The more you allow them to do this, the more they will continue doing it. Invest in people who are willing to invest in you. You shouldn't waste your time and energy trying to make it work with someone who isn't putting the same effort forward. If you have to force it, it probably isn't right. Yes, I know that it's easier said then done, but in truth why sacrifice your happiness and someone else's? It's okay if it doesn't work out with someone. Just learn from that relationship what you don't want in your next one, and don't continue to bring baggage from one relationship to the next so that you continue to make the same mistakes over and over again.

CONNECT WITH LIKE-MINDED PEOPLE

Now that you understand toxic people need to be removed from your life or else they will hold you back, you must learn how to develop relationships with people that will positively impact you. You can start by becoming happier and more excited about your life. The people that are succeeding aren't out there complaining about the way things are, they are making things happen. If your energy state is low and negative, you will repel someone that is a positive influence. These people are glowing and always smiling, and if you come around them while you're in a depressed mood, they will most likely avoid you. They don't allow negative people into their circle of influence because they know the impact it will have on them.

Just smiling can attract people into your life. There have been studies that show smiling will actually change your physiology and make you feel happier. There is a law known as the *Law of Reciprocity*, which is when people feel the need to return whatever you give to them. When you smile at someone, they feel the need to smile back. The same thing happens if you show appreciation to someone. They want to do something to return the favor. If you're looking to attract love into your life, you must first be willing to give love.

Get out there, and go to places where these high-level people are going. They most likely aren't out at the club on the weekend "getting turned up." A good place to find like-minded individuals would be at seminars or local meet-ups. There's an app, *Meetup* (**www.meetup.com**), that you can download for free to help you with this. This is a great way to get out there and start networking. There are also many people connecting through social media platforms; and you can build out your network of friends on there, as well. You can start by adding me through my various accounts. I would love to join your network! I will include all of my links at the end of this chapter.

I highly suggest you start seeking out a mentor or a coach. They should be someone that is already successful in the field you are looking to master. When someone goes to the gym and they have no idea how to exercise, they hire a personal trainer. Getting a coach or mentor is like having a personal trainer for your life. They're someone who will guide you to becoming successful much quicker. Does it make sense to spend the next twenty years trying to figure out everything on your own, when there are plenty of people out there that have already figured these things out and would love to help you? One of the great things about coaches and mentors is that they love to help people. You may have to pay some for their service, but others will give you free valuable insight. Don't go asking someone to be your mentor, before you have built a relationship. This would be like asking a man or woman that you just met in a bar to marry you.

There is a lot of value to be gained by paying for a coaching service. It's an investment in yourself, and with the right coach, it will help you develop much quicker. Find someone that properly aligns with you as a person. A good coach will hold a mirror up to your face and give you direct feedback, whether it's good or bad. They're there to guide you and to hold you accountable, but a coach won't do the work for you. For the coaching to be most effective, you must put forth the effort.

When you meet someone that you think would be good to have in your life, find a way to add value to them immediately. This is one thing that many people don't do, and it's a major gateway for getting someone to like you! If you genuinely seek to add value to someone else's life, no matter what level they are at, they will deeply appreciate it. You can figure out how to do this by simply asking, "Is there anything you are struggling with that I can help you with?" They won't forget this, but only do it if you're being genuine and truly want to add value to that person's life. They will be able to tell if you are being fake about it.

Another great way to build rapport with someone is to listen to them. By listening, you show a genuine interest in that other person. One of the strongest human needs is the need to feel important. When you actually listen and don't just sit there waiting for your turn to talk or rudely interrupt the other person, people appreciate that because everyone wants to be heard. No one is more important to that person than they are to themselves. Here's something to think about. If you were suffering from a migraine and at the same time there was a plague going on in another country, you would most likely be more concerned about your migraine. Keep this in mind when you are in a conversation with someone. Show a genuine interest in that person and seek to add value to their life.

Calling someone by their name will help you to connect closer to them. To them, their name is the most important name on this planet. By saying their name, they instantly are listening because they feel like you know each other. Make sure you remember their name and say it correctly.

Mirroring and matching is another technique you can use to build a closer connection with someone. People like other people who are like them. When you are talking with someone, make an effort to mirror the tone of their voice. If you go into a conversation with someone who is super excited and high energy and you come in quiet and low energy, that person will think there is a problem with you. Matching their tone of voice will establish a connection. This approach will also work to neutralize a situation if someone is yelling at you. If you speak very softly back to them, after 4 or 5 sentences, they will actually begin mirroring your voice.

Physical positioning plays an important role in

connection, as well. Try to position yourself in front of the person because people don't connect well when you are beside them or behind them. When in front of them, use body posture similar to what they are using. Without even noticing it, they will begin to feel like you are more alike. If you're on a date and your date takes a drink out of their glass, you take a drink out of yours. If they cross their arms, you cross yours. These are simple little things, but they work.

If a conversation starts taking a direction you don't want it to, you can shift the direction by breaking the speaker's thought pattern; and you can do this simply by commenting on something completely random going on around you. Once you have broken their pattern, restart the conversation with a new question. The person who asks the most questions controls the tempo of the conversation and learns the most. If you walk into a conversation and talk the entire time, you walk away with the same amount of knowledge. The quality of your questions determines the quality of your life. If you ask someone great questions, not only are you making them feel special but you are gaining insight and more knowledge!

Focus on be interested, not interesting. The more interest you show in the other person, the more they will feel connected to you. A general rule to use is to listen twice as much as you talk. That is why I believe our creator gave us two ears and only one mouth.

Also, keep in mind that your appearance matters. Before you even open your mouth, people are going to naturally judge you based off how you look. Make sure you are dressed for the occasion, and you have proper hygiene. I know this is common practice, but it's not uncommon for people to skip this! This is why it's important to take care of your physical body with proper nutrition and exercise. If you're overweight, people make assumptions that you're not a very disciplined person. Your physical body is a temple, and you really should take great care of it. Next, I'm going to give you a few tips to get you started on becoming healthier and more fit.

MASTER YOUR BODY

If your physical body lacks, it can largely impact your overall wellbeing, and it will make it very difficult to be happy in general. I've experienced this because I was once overweight, and I can tell you that by making some adjustments you too can begin to love your body. If you don't have the energy to get up off the couch to go chase your dreams, it doesn't matter how amazing your vision is. Mastering your body is a fundamental part of your journey to success. When you have low energy, it will be very difficult to keep pushing through challenges or tasks. If your body is not where you want it to be, then it's time to start acting and taking control of it. When it comes to your body composition, your nutrition is a key factor; and exercise contributes only about 20 percent to it. You can't out-train a bad diet, so don't waste your time. I see many people who work really hard at the gym, and then they turn around and ruin all their hard work with the foods they're eating.

You need to become health conscious about the foods you're consuming. Ask yourself questions like, "Is this food clogging me, or cleansing me?" A lot of foods in the American diet are clogging foods; and having so many foods to choose from, as part of this diet, can also be a problem. These foods clog up your blood vessels and arteries, which slows down the flow of nutrients and oxygen being delivered to your vital organs. You should be eliminating or avoiding in excessive amounts: sugar, dairy, sodium, alcohol, drugs, unhealthy oils, and white carbs.

Don't waste your calories by drinking them

away. It's very easy to start drinking more water, instead of high calorie beverages, if you take action to develop the habit. I typically recommend .5 ounces per pound of bodyweight; but if you're an athlete, aim for 1 ounce per pound of body weight instead.

Include as many green vegetables in your diet as possible. I recommend 3-4 daily servings of green vegetables, such as spinach, cucumbers, broccoli, asparagus, kale, or any other green vegetable. I'm a huge fan of plant-based foods because they are nutrient-dense, and our bodies accept those nutrients very well. They also have a lot of fiber and vitamins that your body needs.

Do yourself a favor, and pick up some good quality spices at your local health food store. Some tend to think that eating healthy is boring, but that's only because they don't properly season their food. Some "good" spices that you can use are: basil, parsley, Himalayan pink salt, cracked black pepper, nutritional yeast, cayenne pepper, turmeric, ginger and cinnamon.

It's important to become intuitive with your food. Pay attention to how it makes you feel after you eat it. How does it make your stomach feel? Are you tired afterward? Do you have a headache? Do you feel bloated or inflamed? Observing these things is what I like to call "intuitive eating". Listen to the feedback your body is giving you, based off of the food you are consuming.

When it comes to exercise, start hitting the gym 3-4 times a week. Eventually, you will want to build up to 5-6 times a week. Keep doing this until it becomes a habit. At first it will seem like a struggle, but eventually you will start to love it because it is rewarding to see results. Remember, exercise is only going to compliment your nutrition. If you're bored with doing steady-state cardio, switch it up with some strength training or interval training. You don't need to lift crazy heavy weights to become in good shape. Bodyweight exercises are also challenging, and they are great for sculpting a lean body.

Interval training is one of the best ways to burn fat. A typical interval workout is 15-20 minutes. It's designed to be a short burst of energy with a small resting period. The goal is to elevate your heart rate up and down to confuse your body. An example of an interval workout would be 20 seconds of exercise with a 10 seconds of rest. The exercise is done at a maximum effort, and then you rest. Do multiple rounds of this type of training exercise, and you will have a great workout.

Sleep plays a large role in the energy that you have for the day. This tends to be overlooked because it's so obvious. There are a few ways you can get better sleep to improve your energy.

Here are some suggestions for better sleep:

- Make sure that you sleep in a completely dark room.

- Avoid electronics that project blue light, such as cell phones, computers or televisions, at least an hour before bed. This blue light is harmful to your eyes and makes your body think it's still daytime outside.

- Avoid eating 2-3 hours before you go to sleep. When you eat right before bed, your body stays awake because it is using energy to break down the food you just consumed.

- It helps to have the room at a cooler temperature. This way you aren't overheating when you sleep.

Learning to master your body takes time, patience and effort. It's all worth it because it will increase your levels of confidence when you are meeting new people. On top of that, you will have higher levels of energy to get more done during the day. You are going to need as much energy as possible, if you are intending to succeed in life.

Once you begin networking with like-minded people, you will love that feeling of connection you get with someone who shares the same values and interests; and you'll feel like you have known that person for years. This will only happen when you push yourself out of your comfort zone to meet new people and raise your standards for the people in your circle of influence.

Here are my social media accounts for you to follow and connect with me on:

Facebook: fb.me/jakewoodardinspire

Instagram: Jakewoodard_inspire

YouTube: Jake Woodard

Website: www.jakewoodard.com

YOUR ACTION STEPS FOR THIS CHAPTER:

Write down your answers below or on a separate sheet of paper.

1. Who are five people that you could reach out to right now and
    ask to have coffee with?

_____

_____

_____

_____

_____

_____

What seminar or meet up could you go to within the next three
months to network with new people?

_____

_____

_____

_____

_____

_____

Smile at five random people today, and see if you can get them
to smile back. Yes, I know this is awkward and uncomfortable,
but that means you are growing!

_____

_____

_____

_____

_____

_____

Chapter 6

Creating Your Unstoppable Mindset

"Give me six hours to chop down tree, and I will spend
the first four hours sharpening the axe."
-ABRAHAM LINCOLN

The day my life took a whole new course was
when I decided to pick up the book *Rich Dad, Poor
Dad* by Robert Kiyosaki. I was driving around at my
job and wondering if this was the extent of my life.
Had I done all I was going to do? I began to ask myself a lot of powerful questions like this. All the while
knowing that I wanted more out of life, and that I was
settling. I'd never been the kind of person to settle, so
I decided that I wasn't about to start now. In twenty-
four years, I had never read a book completely. My
lack of patience didn't allow me to do so. When I began reading this book, it was like all of the thoughts
that I had in my head were in the book! This book
spelled out for me the difference between what the

rich teach their kids and what the poor and middle class don't, and as a result I became immediately obsessed with and addicted to personal development.

How many books a year do you read? The average person reads one book a year. While the top earning CEOs, on average, read sixty-plus books a year. It really does speak volumes that readers are leaders. Remember, there are a lot of books out there that you can read. You want to focus on books that will grow your mind strength, such as those focusing on personal development, business, psychology, money or health. It's good to focus on these areas that will actually benefit your life.

It's been said that Warren Buffet, one of the richest men of our time, spends the first five hours of his day reading books. He is considered by some to be one of the most successful investors in the world. He started reading books at the very early age of seven years old. He said it best: "The more you learn, the more you earn." When you read a book, you take in all of the insight that its author learned throughout their journey through life. People who write books love to share the stories of their failures, their successes and all the things they have learned. You can start out small and just read 10 pages of an inspirational book each day. You have to start somewhere, but the point is to start.

WIN THE MORNING, WIN THE DAY

When you wake up in the morning are you scurrying around your house to get ready and rushing out the door? When you start your day out stressful, you are already setting yourself up to have a difficult day. The morning doesn't have to be a disaster, nor should it be; and if you develop a morning routine, it won't be. This practice should be a non-negotiable and essential part of your lifestyle, meaning you do it everyday as a regular part of your life. Many successful people have very strong morning routines, and you can create one that works well for yourself. An ideal morning routine is one that you are going to do and enjoy doing. This isn't some difficult task, look at it as strengthening your mind before you go out into the world. As soon as you walk out your door, you will be ready for whatever challenges the day brings.

Your willpower is the strongest in the morning. It's like your cell phone battery, in the way that the more you use it throughout your day, the more the battery decreases. If you have an important task to get done, do it as soon as you can after waking up. Remember, this is your life, you create it exactly how you want. You want to do what is going to work for your life and enjoyable for you to do or it won't last.

Here are some examples of things you can do as part of your morning routine:

- **Set your alarm across the room with a motivational song to wake up to.** Put the label as something inspirational. For example, "abundance is flowing to you." Our alarm is the first thing we hear in the morning, so why would you want something you don't like?

- **Make your bed.** The reason you do this is because when you come home after a long day you will have a nice clean bed to get into. It is also a small victory in your mind when you see it. You want to create as many small victories as possible throughout your day.

- **Drink cold water.** This helps to hydrate your system because you lose water as you sleep and typically wake up dehydrated!

- **Take a contrast shower.** Take your warm shower with soap, then switch the water to ice cold and stand there for 60 seconds. This is a shock to your body and stimulates your adrenal glands. It helps to wake you up, and it also strengthens your immune system. There is a lot of research about the benefits of cold exposure, if you are interested.

- **Meditate.** Meditation has been around for thousands of years, and it's an amazing way to calm your mind and create peace within your life. It also helps with your ability to focus. If you are new to meditation, you can do a guided meditation. There are many different guided meditations available, and you can find some by simply going on the internet and searching for them. Make sure you do this in a quiet and dark room where you will be able to be in complete stillness.

- **Exercise with stretching and yoga poses.** You can also do foam rolling. By doing exercise in the morning, you are creating energy which will help you feel more energized throughout the day. This will cause an increase in blood flow, which will allow more oxygen and nutrients to be distributed throughout your body.

- **Read.** Sharpen your mind every morning by learning something new. Aim to read a minimum of ten pages out of a self-improvement book. If you can't do ten, then start with just five pages. It won't take very long for you to read a book when you consistently read.

- **Breakfast.** Have breakfast with a lot of green vegetables. It's important to get some good nutrients in your system to supply you with energy. A lot of people say that breakfast is your most important meal of the day, but I believe every meal is equally as important.

Start mapping out what your morning routine looks like. If you have kids, you might have to get up earlier before the rest of the house is awake to make time for yourself. I want you to create what is really going to work for you. Remember that you need to create something that is going to become a regular part of your life, so make it something you enjoy.

Practicing gratitude is another way to develop an unstoppable mindset. At any point in your life, there is always something you can be grateful for. No matter how bad of a day you think you're having, you can always stop and take a moment to be grateful. Gratitude is a very powerful force. It has the ability to change your entire mood just by engaging in things in your life that you are grateful for. The next time you get upset or angry, stop for a moment, close your eyes, and start telling yourself everything you are grateful for. It is not possible for you to be upset and grateful at the same time. These expressions of gratitude can come from the simplest things too, like the warm bed you have to sleep in or the nice meal you had earlier that day.

You are learning how to recondition your current mindset. Every time that you practice one of these, that pattern will become stronger in your mind. The more times you do it, the better you will become at it and the stronger your mind becomes. It's like learning a new language. You didn't start out by being able to speak your new language proficiently. Through many hours of practicing and repeating words, you became better and better at speaking your language.

Eventually, you get to the point where you no longer need to practice. It just becomes natural to you.

You are a combination of the thoughts that you repeatedly have and the actions you consistently take. Developing a positive internal dialogue is done by taking control of your thoughts and becoming aware of them. The power of affirmations is a great way to create new patterns in your mind. They help to reinforce and strengthen new thoughts or ideas that you may have. To some people this may seem a little bizarre, but saying positive words repeatedly out loud has a profound effect on your mindset. Remember, the more you repeat something, the easier and more real it will start becoming. When saying an affirmation, you always want to put "I am" in front of the sentence. This is because your mind only recognizes things in the present state. It doesn't know past or future tense. It's the same thing when you are writing your goals down. You want to write them like they are already happening in your life.

Here are some example affirmations:

- I am successful in all that I do.
- I am totally confident.
- I am very focused and persistent.

- I express my gratitude daily.

- I am always calm, patient and happy.

- Money comes to me with ease.

- I attract all of the right people into my life.

- My health and vitality are forever increasing.

When you say words out loud they register into your subconscious mind. When you continue to repeat the same words, those thoughts become stronger and stronger. This is why your thoughts are creating your physical reality. When you learn to control your thoughts, you can set your mind free. Building confidence is done when you continue to push yourself out of your comfort zone and take on new challenges. Those feelings of insecurity or doubt will start to vanish the more times you do it. You deserve to be confident. You deserve to have an unstoppable mindset.

YOUR ACTION STEPS FOR THIS CHAPTER:

Write your answers below or on a separate sheet of paper.

1. Map out your new morning routine. What does it consist of?

    _____

    _____

    _____

    _____

    _____

    _____

2. What are three new affirmations that you could start saying to yourself or out loud?

    _____

    _____

    _____

    _____

    _____

    _____

3. What book are you going to start reading?

    _____

    _____

    _____

    _____

    _____

    _____

CHAPTER 7

Finding Your Purpose

Finding your life's purpose can be very challenging and can take some real soul searching, but it's essential that you identify it. In order to do this, you must start with your "why". Why you want to make a difference in our world. Why you want to become successful. Why you want to live a better life. Create a clear and compelling purpose by identifying your reasoning for why you want what you desire. It may seem fuzzy and unclear when you think about what your future looks like. That is totally fine. The more you start to tap into your mission in life, the more clear it will become. We all have a purpose for being here. Each and everyone of us has gifts and abilities to share with the world.

Are you too afraid of trying to find your purpose because you don't think you are ready yet? If you sit back and never take action, you will continue searching your entire life. The timing will never be just right. By simply taking action, you will start to gain momentum along the way. This will also help to bring you clarity. If you were to take a trip in your car and wait for all of the lights to turn green before you left your house, you would most likely never leave your house. You are going to hit red lights along your path in life. Those red lights are put in place to challenge you so that you will continue to grow. No one ever becomes great in life without facing challenges or adversity along the way. That is a part of the process to discovering what you were meant to do in life. Understand that perfection doesn't exist, and it's just an excuse to procrastinate. If you consider yourself a perfectionist, you are now what I call a "recovering perfectionist." Now that you know perfection doesn't exist, don't let the fear of not achieving it hold you back. You will become the best version of you.

BUILDING MOMENTUM

Henry Ford said it best: "When everything seems

to be going against you, remember the airplane takes off against the wind, not with it." It will be helpful to keep this in mind, as you are bound to face a lot of resistance when you are starting to discover your life's purpose. You will be up against a society that wants you to stay routine, mediocre or average. People are going to start to look at you differently for chasing your dreams and passion. You might even have people close to you try to talk you out of pursuing your dreams. They will tell you that you can't do something only because they believe they can't do it. Your dreams and vision will make those around you feel weak inside because it's showing them what they gave up on or never created in their own life.

This is why you must discover your purpose. Every time you face resistance or something hard, you will be able to look back at why you started in the first place. People that don't identify a strong enough purpose give up when things start to become difficult. They give up when they get rejected or become uncomfortable in a situation. When you make this message clear and easy to define, your path starts to become more visible. Doors of opportunity that were never there before start to open. Once you begin putting your message out there, you'll see how the universe has a unique way of helping those with a strong purpose in life. Remember, those that chase their dreams in life are rewarded the most. Making this discovery is really about trial and error. You aren't going to like everything you do, but the only person who's going to make this discovery is you. In order to figure out what you do or don't like, you have to try different things.

It is easy for a person to become comfortable or complacent in life; and when they do, they stop growing and evolving. I don't believe you're a person who wants to settle, if this is the type of book you are interested in reading. I believe that you want more out of your life, and that's a good thing. Keep that level of hunger. When you stay hungry and keep searching for answers, they will come.

You always want to be growing and learning, even if it's just a little bit each day. Those who become life-long students live the best lives. They make the most money, have the best experiences and feel fulfilled with their life. If I gave you a billion dollars and I told you that the only way you can keep this money was to go live on an island all by yourself for the rest of your life, would that money bring you happiness? I'm gonna guess that your answer is, "no," and you would feel pretty unfulfilled. When you realize that money alone can't bring you happiness, you start to search for other things. Money is definitely important in life, but it's only a vehicle to have more experiences and help more people. Finding your purpose is really about aligning with what makes you feel happy. What is it that is going to bring you lasting fulfillment? Most of our society does things that they aren't happy doing. They go to a job that they aren't happy with. They stay in a relationship that longer brings them joy. They live in a location that they don't like. I'm telling you right now that you don't have to settle for doing things you consistently don't enjoy.

Your purpose will become more like your calling in life. It's not something that you will be doing for money or significance. If you align strongly with your purpose, all of those things will come naturally as a part of it. I believe that we all have a greater purpose for being here. This becomes clear when we start listening to our intuition. I'm sure that you've heard it at one point or another, but have you ever really listened to it? For example, that feeling that you get in your stomach when you become fearful or when you get butterflies because you are excited about something. Have you ever noticed when someone walks into a room in a bad mood that you can instantly feel their negative energy? This is your intuition, and it's constantly working. It's really important for you to listen to what your body is telling you because your mind is too clouded with thinking to make rational decisions all of the time. If you continuously "feel" like something is wrong in a situation, then it probably is. Maybe you have heard this referred to as a "hunch." Don't ignore that feeling in your gut.

> "Your time is limited, so don't waste it living someone else's life. Don't be trapped by dogma—which is living with the results of other people's thinking. Don't let the noise of other's opinions drown out your own inner voice. And most important, have the courage to follow your heart and intuition. They somehow already know what you truly want to become. Everything else is secondary."
>
> -STEVE JOBS

Knowing exactly what you want out of life isn't about what you get, it's about who you become during the process of discovery. If you relentlessly pursue your dreams and passion, you will—without a doubt—have a break through at some point. It may feel at times like you aren't making any progress, but it's important that you don't give up. It's not uncommon for people to quit too soon, either before they discover their purpose or when they get distracted by something else. When you set out to find your purpose, start by simply thinking about who you would like to become—not what your job title is or what society labels you as. It's not about what degrees or certifications you obtain. Focus on the person you are striving to become each and every day. Start thinking about what type of impact you want to have on our world, and begin to seek answers on how to create the vehicle that is going to drive you there.

When you were a little kid, what did you dream of becoming when you grew up? Have you allowed fear or social conditioning to kill the dream that is deep inside of you? When we are young, we are dreamers because we are fearless. We dared to dream, but as we grow older there are many outside forces that condition us to believe that we shouldn't dream because "those dreams aren't possible." Don't be afraid to start questioning things that you think differently about. Allow yourself to be a dreamer, and start taking action on those dreams that you have.

There are many one-size-fits-all programs for people who don't know what they want in life, such as, "Go to school, get a job and climb the corporate ladder." Does this sound familiar? I say, why not build your own dream life or business and own the corporate ladder? Your life is not a one-size-fits-all hat. You need to spend some time designing your life and building your dreams. If you don't, someone will hire you to help them build their dreams. I know you're probably thinking that we all have to start somewhere in life and work our way up, but that doesn't mean you can't define your purpose and start to gear yourself toward living life on your terms. Imagine what it would feel like to wake up everyday and live a life where you didn't have to answer to a boss or co-workers that you don't get along with or go to a job that isn't fulfilling to you. This all is possible if you're able to clearly identify what you want out of life and are willing to define your purpose.

Developing your patience muscle is going to be a key factor when looking to change your life. You must understand that lasting change won't happen overnight. We all struggle and feel the same pains, and we all face resistance and go through things that are challenging to us. That is all part of the process, and you should learn to enjoy it because to experience growth is very exciting and rewarding.

There is a lot of noise in today's world, and this is why it is crucial that you stay focused on your journey and continue to better yourself each and everyday. The only person that you should be in competition with is the person that you were yesterday. Your continuous investment in yourself will pay huge dividends down the road. It is the best investment you will ever make.

YOUR ACTION STEPS FOR THIS CHAPTER:

Write your answers below or on a separate sheet of paper.

1. What are three steps you are going to take today to start gaining clarity on your purpose?

_____

_____

_____

_____

_____

2. Take a look at where you are in your life right now; and ask yourself can I do more, can I be more, can I have more impact?

_____

_____

_____

_____

_____

3. What dreams or ideas have you had that you aren't taking action on?

_____

_____

_____

_____

_____

CHAPTER 8

A Life of Service

"Be the change you wish to see in the world."
-MAHATMA GHANDI

Have you ever helped someone that you felt had nothing they could possibly give back to you? Did the feelings of warmth and happiness flood your heart, as you walked away from them? Being of service to others is a powerful way to live your life. In order to live an abundant life, you must first be willing to give back without the intention of getting something out of it. When you give with no intention of receiving, you will be rewarded heavily at some point in your life. There are universal laws that govern the act of giving to those in need. This doesn't necessarily mean giving money to a homeless person. You will discover your own ways of giving back, once you find the gifts you already have within you to share.

Out of everything I have done so far in life, giving back and helping others has brought me more gratification than anything else. When you give to someone that doesn't have the ability to pay you or give you anything back, it warms your heart. Your reward is knowing that you made a difference in that person's life just by being genuine. When you set out to help others and be of service, your life will feel like it has more purpose and meaning.

Allow me to share with you an example story of giving back. I was once at a professional baseball game and spotted a custodian that seemed like he was a little down. I walked over to the man, as he was sweeping up trash, and said, "Excuse me, sir." He looked up with sadness in his face. I said, "Has anyone told you lately that they appreciate you?" He didn't speak English very well, so I placed my hand over my heart and then on his and said the words, "I appreciate you." His face brightened with joy, and then tears came to his eyes. It was as if no one in his life had ever said those words to him before. I walked by him again later, but this time as he continued to sweep up trash, he was singing and dancing around. That transaction took only about 30 seconds of my time, but it's a perfect example of how it doesn't take a lot to make someone else's day. I believe that everyone wants to feel appreciated and loved. People will work harder for appreciation and praise than they will for money itself. Think about this the next time someone does something for you. Don't be afraid to show them appreciation or tell them how great they are at something. Who knows the impact it could have on that person's life. You never know what a person is dealing with or going through. Everyone is facing different struggles, and by you showing them that you genuinely care, you might change their entire mood. It could even change their life.

How are you showing up in society? Do you only do things that you get paid for, or are you out there adding as much value to people as you possibly can? When you begin adding real value to people's lives, it changes the quality of your own life. You will feel like you are beginning to make a difference in our world. Zig Ziglar said it best: "You can have everything you want in life, if you just help enough other people get what they want."

One of the reasons I created a non-profit organization was to make a difference in our world. This is something that I'm very proud of and hold dear to my heart. **The Family Time Inc.** was formed to provide underprivileged children with toys on Christmas. We also provide meals to those in need on Thanksgiving. The reason for doing this was to help bring families closer together and show them that people care.

Not everyone is given the same opportunities in life, and some people really are dealt a bad hand. Understand how fortunate you are to have the life you do. If you have a roof over your head, food in your fridge and a warm bed to sleep in then you are more blessed than a lot of the world's population. The fact that you even have clean water to drink in itself is amazing. Almost one billion people don't have access to clean water, and almost 2.5 billion people don't have access to adequate sanitation. You know how bad your life becomes when the power goes out for a few days. Imagine living in an environment with no electricity or running water. Would you still complain about the little things that go wrong in your life, like having to wait in line at a drive-thru restaurant?

It's very easy to take things for granted in life, until they are taken away from you. We typically don't miss something until it's gone. This is called the *Law of Familiarity*. When you become familiar with something, you start to take it for granted and expect it to always be there. Don't take anything for granted because it could be gone tomorrow. This goes for all aspects of your life. When you start looking at things in their proper perspective, like that your situation could always be worse—much, much worse—life doesn't seem so bad, and you really do become grateful for all that you have. Think about all that you have to give right now. You may be thinking, "Well, I don't have any money to give," but you probably could spare a dollar. The next time you're buying a $170 pair of shoes and you get a chance to donate at the cash register, think about that. Those who give the most and do the most for others, live the best lives.

When you are introduced to someone new, a great way to tell the kind of person they are is by watching how they treat other people. If you are at a restaurant and they treat a waiter poorly, it's a good indicator of how they treat everyone. The way you do one thing, is the way you do everything. That's why it's important to always hold your same standards level no matter who you are engaging with. Treat a janitor with the same level of respect as you would a CEO. Why? Because who are you to judge someone based on their job description. It doesn't identify their personality, and you should treat them equally. It's so easy to simply make someone's day by showing them your appreciation for what they do. They might even begin to do it better and with more passion after you acknowledge their efforts.

Imagine how much better our world would be if everyone started to shift their thinking to being of service to others or stopped always looking to receive and started finding ways to help those around us. When you come from a position of love and have a genuine interest in helping other people, not only does your life get better, but you begin to have a positive impact on our world. It may seem like an impossible task for one person to change the world; but if everyone starts to contribute, it can be done.

Have you ever held the door for a stranger and gotten upset when they didn't say thank you for your kind gesture? I agree that it is rude of that person to not acknowledge you, but when you give with expecting something in return that's what happens. This is because when you have expectations people will let you down. You cannot give something and expect to get something out of it. Anything that you get back is just an added bonus. You have to have the intention of giving just to give and not look for the incentive. Replace any expectations that you have with appreciation. You go to work and expect a paycheck at the end of your work week because you gave them your time and energy. My question for you is this. What are you doing outside of your work to really help others? It's not necessary to always be compensated for helping people. Often times, when you help someone out the most, it's when the person cannot repay you. It's the simple act of you wanting to help someone that is the rewarding part.

Here are some examples of things you can do to start giving back:

- Find a charity that you like and donate your time or money to it.

- Tell a random person, such as a cashier or a janitor, that you appreciate their service.

- Give a random compliment to a stranger.

- Figure out a way you can help the youth.

- Go to a retirement home to sit and talk with the elders.

There are many charitable organizations out there you could get involved with. Find one that aligns with your values. You don't even have to give money. You can donate some of your time. You will be amazed at the responses you get from people when you give them your appreciation or a compliment.

Some may think it's strange, but others may deeply appreciate it. It's very important to have fun with it and come from a place of authenticity. Sitting and talking to older people about their lives is always interesting. They get lonely, and they just want to share their stories with someone. It's a great way for you to practice your listening skills, and you will make someone's day in the process. Albert Einstein said, "Strive not to be a success, but rather to be of value." No one really cares how successful you are. They remember a person by how much value they added to those around them.

You never know the impact that you could have on just one person. You could change someone's life forever, and they could go on to inspire millions of people. Maybe they will become a scientist who discovers a new cure for an incurable disease. This is all because you showed an interest to help someone and that you took the time and invested it making our world a better place.

YOUR ACTION STEPS FOR THIS CHAPTER:

Write your answers below or on a separate sheet of paper.

1. Who is someone that you believe needs your help right now?

_____

_____

_____

_____

_____

_____

_____

2. I challenge you to compliment or show appreciation to a random person within the next week.

_____

_____

_____

_____

_____

_____

3. What value do you intend on adding to the world?

_____

_____

_____

_____

_____

_____

Chapter 9

Creating Your Legacy

"I've learned that people will forget what you said, people will forget what you did, but people will never forget how you made them feel."
-MAYA ANGELOU

How is it that you want to be remembered? If someone two hundred years from now were to pick up a book written about your life, would they want to read it, or would they get through the first chapter and throw the book away? I want you to start thinking about the legacy that you are creating, today. Your story is being written every moment that you are alive. When you wake up in the morning, instead of hitting the snooze alarm multiple times, think of how you will conquer the day. Start to think about all of the amazing things that you are going to manifest into your life, the opportunity that is going to come your way, and if it doesn't, how you will create it. When you have created a compelling vision and know your life's purpose, it will be much easier to leave behind your legacy. Everything you have ever desired will become a part of your life.

I know that it's difficult to be patient and wait for things to start happening, but it will be well worth it. Imagine how much you could accomplish in the next five years of continuous learning and growing everyday? Even if it's just a small amount, keep making those deposits into your mental bank account. The return on that investment will be a life of happiness, fulfillment and abundance. If you wait a year from now to take action, then you will wish that you had started today. You will never have all of the answers, but it's important that you take that first step. You no longer need to stay at a job you hate, date someone that you don't enjoy being with or live somewhere you don't like. Your problem may just be the way you think and the way you see the world around you. No matter what your physical environment is, if you want to live a great life you must have a beautiful internal environment.

Become the type of person that has so much mental strength that you don't allow little things to bother you. There will always be things in your life that pop up and try to distract you or hold you back. Be aware of the shiny objects that you are chasing in your life. This can be people, cars, money or even a result that you think will bring you fulfillment.

Understand that creating a legacy is something that will last forever. Think about all of the great people in history that stood for something and will never be forgotten. These people changed the course of the world forever because they were willing to take action and stand up for what they believed in. They didn't allow fear, failure or rejection to stop them from making their dreams come true and leaving a legacy.

Let me share with you some quotes from people who changed our world.

"You will find men who want to be carried on the shoulders of others, who think that the world owes them a living. They don't seem to see that we must all lift together and pull together."
- HENRY FORD

"I learned that courage was not the absence of fear, but the triumph over it. The brave man is not he who does not feel afraid, but he who conquers that fear."
- NELSON MANDELA

"It is not how much we do, but how much love we put in the doing. It is not how much we give, but how much love we put in the giving."
– MOTHER TERESA

I know some people might not care about creating a legacy, and they may be happy with their mediocre lifestyle; but if you want more out of your life and you want to achieve a legacy and greatness, you must be willing to go through the process. You will have to start thinking differently than other people, come up with your own beliefs and start questioning what society has conditioned you to believe. It's okay to think differently. As long as you believe in yourself, then nothing else matters. You don't need validation from anyone other than yourself. It doesn't matter if you fail because you will learn from your failures and keep moving forward.

Understand that you have the power of choice. You cannot control what problems show up in your life, but you can choose how you respond to them. You have complete control over your attitude and the way you view things. It's how you choose to think about what is happening that will determine your outcome. When you get positive results, that's because you had a positive attitude towards what you were doing. You become the thoughts that you have continuously. If you are choosing to stay at a job you hate, that is your choice. If you choose to be with someone you don't enjoy being with, that is your choice. If you choose to eat unhealthy and be overweight, that is your choice. I believe you understand that you have the power to make better choices. If you aren't happy with your current circumstances in life, simply choose to change them.

Everyone is at a different point in their journey. It's important that you don't get caught up comparing yourself to someone else. If someone has been diligently working at something for ten years, then of course, they are going to be farther along then you are.

I truly believe that every person is capable of creating their own legacy. We all have gifts and abilities to share with the world. Scientists estimate the probability of you being born is about 1 in 400 trillion. The chances of you getting struck by lightning are about 1 in 12,000. I would say, with the comparison of those odds, that makes you an absolute miracle. The next time you don't feel special, I want you to think about those odds. If you tell me that you don't think you were born for a much larger purpose, then I would have to disagree with you.

Don't ever let someone else tell you your worth. This will not only help you with your financial life, but it will also help with your relationships. You want to be able to clearly identify your own value and self-worth. If you don't, then people will try to take advantage of you. Don't allow your kindness to be a weakness. It's easy for us to overestimate other people and underestimate ourselves. You can see a person who is a millionaire and automatically think they must be superhuman. Not so. They are no better than you or I. They have just managed to amass a lot of money in their life. A job title, bank account or social status doesn't define a person. No one will meaningfully remember you by the amount of material things or money that you acquired in your life. People remember the impact that you had on the world and the things you did for others while you were here.

Be selective about who you choose to take advice from. It's important that you learn to filter out bad information because there is a lot of it out there in today's world. Everyone can go on the internet and have an opinion. Only listen to those who are actually out there taking action, having impact and making our world a better place. People will only understand you from their own level of perception. This means, if you have a big vision and the person you are talking to doesn't, they will most likely disagree with you and tell you it can't be done. I do believe that there's also a lot of good advice out there, as well. Coaches and mentors have helped me immensely in my life. They help you to create a roadmap that guides you on your journey.

If there were a survey that asked people what they wanted most out of life, their responses would be something like this. Most would say, "I don't know." A few would say some generic response like, "happiness" or "financial freedom." Even fewer would be able to give you a clear definition of their life's purpose. Those few that can define their life's purpose are the one's that successfully create a legacy and change our world. Become clear on your life's purpose, so you too can achieve greatness.

I know you want to live a better life and you can, but that only happens if you believe you can. You can read all of the books, attend all of the seminars and buy every course; but if you don't believe that you have what it takes, then you will never take action. In order for you start living life on your terms, you have to start executing action steps. Lay out your vision and goals of what your future is going to be. Most people spend more time planning out their Christmas vacation then they do planning out their lives.

There are those who live for the weekends, and there those who live for every day they wake up.

There are 86,400 seconds in a day. How you spend your time is going to determine how successful you become. We all have the same 24 hours in a day. Your time is your biggest asset, and it is one of the few things you cannot create more of. How are you going to start spending those 24 hours?

YOUR ACTION STEPS FOR THIS CHAPTER:

Write your answers below or on a separate sheet of paper.

1. What legacy are you going to create?

    Example: I, (your name), am going to create...

    _____

    _____

    _____

2. How do you want to be remembered?

    _____

    _____

    _____

    _____

3. What steps are you going to take to start best utilizing your time?

    _____

    _____

    _____

    _____

Closing Words

I want to sincerely thank you for taking the time to read this book. My hope is that I have opened your eyes to a new way of viewing the world. If you had some "ah-ha" moments or shifts in your thinking, feel free to post them on social media or send me an email. I would love to hear about them. My passion is helping people realize the gifts within them and that they too can share them with the world. Who knows, maybe now you can write a book, or go out and start having your own impact on our world.

Acknowledgements

I would like to acknowledge and thank my family: my mother, Paula Woodard, who has blessed me with unconditional love; my father, Ken Woodard, who has shown me an amazing work ethic; and my younger sister, Jasmine Woodard, who has always stood by my side through the good and the bad.

I'm grateful for the mentors that have come into my life along the way. A special thanks to Curtis Lewsey, Josh Dulmer, Rod Khleif, Matt Stone, Dave Lopez, Steve Gallegos and many more.

An additional special thanks goes to Joy Dilworth for helping me to bring this book to life. Your attention to detail and creative eye are phenomenal.

A very special thanks goes to Nina Munoz for helping me learn balance and patience. Your beautiful energy is appreciated.

I also appreciate all of the people who I inspire through my life's mission. Without you, I wouldn't have much purpose to keep developing myself and finding new ways to give back. It has been an amazing journey, thus far, and I'm only just beginning. Thank you, and I love you all.

Follow and connect with the author:

Facebook: fb.me/jakewoodardinspire

Instagram: Jakewoodard_inspire

YouTube: Jake Woodard

Website: www.jakewoodard.com

Made in the USA
Lexington, KY
24 October 2017